George Pennington

Little Manual for Players of the Glass Bead Game

The Way of Visual Contemplation

Element Books

© Element Books Ltd 1983

First published in 1981 by Irisiana Verlag
Haldenwang, West Germany
First published in Great Britain by
Element Books, The Old Brewery, Tisbury, Wiltshire

Designed by Humphrey Stone
Printed by Robert Hartnoll Ltd, Bodmin, Cornwall

ISBN 0 906540 30 5

Contents

Introduction

    What it's about . . . 7

Exercises

    A beginner's tale 20
    Soft vision 24
    Looking nowhere – seeing everything 29
    Double thumbs 32
    One double thumb 35
    Exercise for the weaker (non-dominant) eye 38
    Four thumbs 41
    The middle thumb 43
    Large thumb – small thumb 47
    Red circle – blue circle 50
    Three-dimensional vision – for those who do not know it 54
    Curved space 57
    Hints 60

Contemplation of the Ten Thousand Things   63

2 + 2, A Glass Bead Game for Beginners   65

Notes and references   110

My eyes wide open
in astonishment and wonder
I bow to Him who knows and guides the flow
and stay content
to be just what I am:
a man —

Introduction

What it's about . . .

The Tao that can be told is not the eternal Tao.
The name that can be named is not the eternal name.
The nameless is the beginning of heaven and earth.
The named is the mother of ten thousand things.[1]

There are many things I can talk and write about easily. Everyday things. Things I know, which my rational mind can understand. Language, as I have learned it, is well suited for labelling and communicating these things. Language is essentially the expression of my knowledge and intelligence.

Here, however, we are not concerned with either knowledge or intelligence. Hermann Hesse's Glass Bead Game has little to do with these things either. Here we are dealing with an experience – an experience which lies beyond our everyday world, beyond the scope of our knowledge and intelligence.

This experience is 'nameless'. There are no words to describe it. Anyone who wishes to say something about it has to make do with our ordinary language – a language which is foreign to it. It is like trying to express the experience of a sunrise in mathematical symbols. Such endeavours usually result in images and parables. The Tao (the Way or Path) and the Glass Bead Game are typical examples of such images; they point essentially to one and the same thing.

I was faced with the same difficulty in writing this book. I can say nothing about the essence of my 'subject matter'. That essence is the spiritual foundation of our human existence. Not as a theory but as an experience. And for that experience I have no words.

Consequently, this book speaks in images and parables. They all point to an experience which anyone who wishes can have. Above all, they point out a way which can lead to the experience. They point to the Glass Bead Game itself.

What is the Glass Bead Game? Hermann Hesse, who originated the expression, tells us nothing about the details, nothing about the experience of the Game. He does, however, talk about its nature:

> *I suddenly realized that in the language, or at any rate in the spirit of the Glass Bead Game, everything was actually all-meaningful, that every symbol and combination of symbols led not hither and yon, not to single examples, experiments and proofs, but into the centre, the mystery and innermost heart of the world, into primal knowledge.*[2]

Only a short while ago, I realized how much this and similar allusions have influenced me. Looking back, I can see that my entire development over the past fifteen years has been directed towards unveiling the secret of the Glass Bead Game. It was a strangely confused and adventurous path, yet I never lost sight of the focus of my search, even though I could not have formulated it clearly at the time. And today I know that even the rest of my life will not suffice to fathom the depths of this Game.

And the serpent said unto the woman, Ye shall not surely die: For God doth know that in the day ye eat thereof, then your eyes shall be opened, and ye shall be as gods, knowing good and evil.[3]

The Game inevitably begins with the fall from grace, the loss of innocence brought out by tasting the forbidden fruit, the knowledge of good and evil. For as long as we do not start asking questions, we live like children, in a state of innocence, in paradise. We are at one with the world and do not question it.

They are not decent, good and noble; they are selfish, lustful, overbearing, and wrathful, but in reality and at bottom they are innocent, innocent in the same way as children.[2]

As soon as the first question is asked, we move from the original state of unity to that of duality. The separation of subject and object begins. Paradise is lost. Adam feels naked.

We are the real sinners, we who know and think, who have eaten of the Tree of Knowledge . . .[2]

The path through duality is familiar enough. Instead of the satisfying answers we had hoped for, each question answered only brings more questions. No sooner is an answer found than it is overturned. Again and again, we are faced with the question of meaning. And here too – especially here – the answers are unsatisfactory. Basically, we are always searching for the one question to which there is only one answer – and no further questions. It is the search for Paradise Lost.[4]

For Hesse, the Glass Bead Game is a symbol for the path to the lost paradise:

> *It represented an elite, symbolic form of seeking for perfection, a sublime alchemy, an approach to that Mind which beyond all images and multiplicities is one within itself – in other words, to God.*[2]

It is a symbolic expression for the path along which humanity is evolving, for the path which is open to all of us if we are willing to take it. Hesse calls it 'The Game of Games' and 'The path from becoming to being, from the possible to the real.'

The word 'game' is misleading. In Hesse's book, it is quite clear that Joseph Knecht does not merely play a game – for his own entertainment or spiritual edification – but that in the 'playing' he has set out on a path which he will never leave until he dies. It means more than just an amusing, symbolic representation of a path leading to reunion with God (Self-realization, Tao, or whatever else one may choose to call it); it means actually treading the path oneself. 'From becoming to being, from the possible to the real.' This means active realization of our human potential, active evolution.[5]

The version of the Glass Bead Game which I present here is also more than a game. Certainly, those who seek entertainment in it will find it. Intellectual curiosity or sensationalism can also be gratified. Some may be enthusiastic, others indignant. But those who do practise it will discover that it turns eventually into a path of the kind described above.

There are three parts to this Game: Exercises, Contemplation of the Ten Thousand Things and A Glass Bead Game for Beginners. 2 + 2, the Game, is a symbolic and analogic representation of the process set in motion by the Exercises and the Contemplation which comprise the actual path.

The main vehicle of the Game is perception. Anyone practising the exercises will find that their perception gradually ceases to fixate on external objects. Indeed, that perception starts to become itself the object of perception, i.e. it becomes its own object. All that is perceived, even perception itself, turns into a mirror.

> *It is not speech which we should want to know:*
> *we should know the speaker.*
> *It is not things seen which we should want to know:*
> *we should know the seer.*
> *It is not sounds which we should want to know:*
> *we should know the hearer.*
> *It is not mind which we should want to know:*
> *we should know the thinker.*[6]

In ancient Egypt, the mirror was not only the symbol for 'life' but also the key to the beyond, the realm of souls (*ankh*). Buddhist tradition often speaks of the 'clear mirror'. Tungu shamans use a magic mirror to 'see the world', to 'place the spirits' or to 'reflect the needs of mankind.'[7] The magician, John Dee, employed a piece of carbon crystal in much the same way, as did the witches in the Middle Ages whose tradition of clairvoyance, using mirrors and crystal balls, is still alive today.

Our legends and fairy tales, too, are full of stories in which mirrors play an important part. Faust's magic mirror is one example. In *Snow White*, the wicked queen causes all kinds of mischief because she cannot bear the truth spoken by her mirror. Atréju, the hero of *The Endless Tale*[8], fares much better. In the course of his adventures and ordeals, he comes to the Magic Mirror Gate and sees in it his true inner essence. Unlike the wicked queen, he is able to accept what he sees and is allowed to pass through the mirror. On the other side, he then meets the Voice Of Silence – but not until he has first passed through the Door Without Key (the *Mu-mon-kan* of Zen).

The story of Hui Neng, the sixth patriarch of Chinese Buddhism, also demonstrates the importance of the mirror for those on the Path. When the fifth patriarch began to look for a successor to his office, Hui Neng was an illiterate lay brother, a helper in the monastery kitchen. A monk named Shen-hsiu, who wanted very much to qualify for the office, wrote the following verse on a wall:

The body is the Bodhi Tree,
The mind like a bright mirror standing.
Take care to wipe it all the time
And allow no dust to cling.

When Hui Neng heard of this verse, he asked another monk to write one on the wall for him:

There never was a Bodhi Tree,
Nor bright mirror standing.
Fundamentally, not one thing exists,
So where is the dust to cling?[9]

While Shen-hsiu is still busy polishing his mirror, Hui Neng has become One with himself. The mirror has gone.

The Glass Bead Game, as I present it here – particularly the Exercises and Contemplation of the Ten Thousand Things – is just such a mirror. The most important advice is simply to contemplate the image that the mirror reflects, *sine ira et studio*, without the anger of the wicked queen or the zeal of Shen-hsiu.

It seems to be much easier for Orientals than for most Westerners to sit in contemplation over long periods of time. Few Europeans can find the external and internal calm which is the prerequisite for sitting Zen meditation. I, too, have always found it difficult, often impossible, to remain anchored in the Here-and-Now – or even to find my way back to it each time I have drifted off into my daydreams during meditation.

Here it is different. In this contemplation we have two anchors, one internal and one external. The latter is an image upon which the eyes rest. They contemplate an object which does not exist, seeing it in a place where there is clearly nothing existing. The eyes are thus looking at a visual manifestation of Nothing, of the Void. Therefore, anything that happens during contemplation is experienced in relation to the Void.

Those for whom the first – and, in my eyes, the most important – exercise has become second nature will have an internal anchor in their physical sensations, such as breathing, heartbeat, sensations in arms and legs, etc. This internal anchor forms a link of awareness to the physical world, the Something, while the external anchor forms a corresponding link with the Nothing, the Void. And it is in the space between these two anchors that the 'clear mirror' – which reflects our own true nature and that of the world around us – emerges.

> *How grateful I am!*
> *This eye of Saichi is the borderline*
> *between this world and the land of peace.*
> *Namu-amida-butsu! Namu-amida-butsu!*[10]

I find it difficult to say much more. A practical attempt means more than a thousand words of explanation.

I feel a deep gratitude for all the people I have met on the Path. I can only name a few here – my great signposts and milestones. The kitchen-boy, Hui Neng, with his poem; and Heinrich von Kleist who opened my eyes with just a few pages – 'On The Puppet Theatre'. [11] (I am still not sure whether he saw himself what he showed me.) Also Gustav Meyrink, who found so many different ways of expressing the same thing – always the same –without ever giving it a name; he, too, was a player of the Glass Bead Game. Then Carlos Castaneda, treading the Path with endearing naivety – feeling his way in the dark. And Pierre Derlon, whose book 'The Gardens of Initiation'[12] made me realize for the first time what I was really doing with my eyes. There are many people without whom I could never have written this book; above all – and here he stands for all the others – Hermann Hesse, who turned my world into a 'Magic Theatre'.

In word, in image, in act, all these blessed souls who kept me company have testified to the eternal reality of their vision. Their everyday world will one day become ours. It is ours now, in fact, only we are too impoverished to claim it for our own. [13]

Exercises

A beginner's tale

He led me to a place where there were two peaks the size of a man standing parallel to each other, about four or five feet apart. Don Juan stopped ten yards away from them, facing the west. He marked a spot for me to stand on and told me to look at the shadows of the peaks. He said that I should watch them and cross my eyes in the same manner I ordinarily crossed them when scanning the ground for a place to rest. He clarified his directions by saying that when searching for a resting place one had to look without focusing but in observing shadows one had to cross the eyes and yet keep a sharp image in focus. The idea was to let one shadow be superimposed on the other by crossing the eyes. He explained that through that process one could ascertain a certain feeling which emanated from the shadows. I commented on his vagueness, but he maintained that there was really no way of describing what he meant.

My attempt to carry out the exercise was futile. Don Juan was not at all concerned with my failure. He climbed to a domelike peak and yelled from the top, telling me to look for two small long and narrow pieces of rock. He showed with his hands the size of rock he wanted.

I found two pieces and handed them to him. Don Juan placed each rock about a foot apart in two crevices, made me stand above them facing the west, and told me to do the same exercise with their shadows.

This time it was an altogether different affair. Almost immediately I was capable of crossing my eyes and perceiving their individual shadows as if they had merged into one. I noticed that the act of looking without converging the images gave the single shadow I had formed an unbelievable depth and a sort of transparency. I stared at it, bewildered. Every hole in the rock, on the area where my eyes were focused, was neatly discernible; and the composite shadow, which was superimposed on them, was like a film of indescribable transparency.

I did not want to blink, for fear of losing the image I was so precariously holding. Finally my sore eyes forced me to blink, but I did not lose the view of the detail at all. In fact, by remoistening my cornea the image became even clearer. I noticed at that point that it was as if I were looking from an immeasurable height at a world I had never seen before. I also noticed that I could scan the surroundings of the shadow without losing the focus of my visual perception. Then, for an instant, I lost the notion that I was looking at a rock.

I felt that I was landing in a world, vast beyond anything I had ever conceived. This extraordinary perception lasted for a second and then everything was turned off. I looked up and saw Don Juan standing directly above the rocks, facing me. He had blocked the sunlight with his body.[14]

Since we need to be anchored with our eyes and consciousness in the Here-and-Now, it is essential that we experience the individual elements of perception consciously, learning to differentiate between them and to open them – in a relaxed way – to the influence of our will. The exercises are a means to this end. They make the anchoring of consciousness – both in the Something and in the Nothing, or, as Saichi says, in 'this world' and in 'the land of peace' – not only possible but playfully simple, and, after a while, quite natural.

The exercises listed are by no means a complete course. There is such an abundance of possible experiences realizable in our consciousness that there can be no such thing as completeness.

The exercises are simply a basis – a means of awakening the curiosity of the person practising them, encouraging him or her to go on and explore the wealth and immensity of consciousness.

Soft vision

At the beginning of our association Don Juan had delineated another procedure: walking for long stretches without focusing the eyes on anything. His recommendation had been to not look at anything directly but, by slightly crossing the eyes, to keep a peripheral view of everything that presented itself to the eyes. He had insisted, although I had not understood at the time, that if one kept one's unfocused eyes at a point just above the horizon, it was possible to notice, at once, everything in almost the total 180-degree range in front of one's eyes. He had assured me that that exercise was the only way of shutting off the internal dialogue. [15]

Sit comfortably in a good light which is neither too bright nor too rich in contrast. Allow your eyes to rest on an object in front of you. Stretch out your arms, parallel in front of you and raised to the level of your eyes, so that your hands frame the object you are looking at on both sides (without concealing it). Keeping your eyes steadily resting on the object, slowly move your hands apart in a wide semicircle – the right hand to the right, the left hand to the left.

Your awareness will now disengage from the direction of your gaze and follow your hands to the outermost limits of your visual field. All the objects across which your hands pass are taken in by your awareness until it finally embraces your entire field of vision. This should be an angle of about 210°.[16]

This procedure will make your vision softer; everything remains fairly clear, without being piercingly sharp. Your expanded awareness through vision is further enriched as your acoustic perception widens and softens in the same way. So it is also through perception of other bodily sensations – breathing, heartbeat, and many others which you would not ordinarily notice.

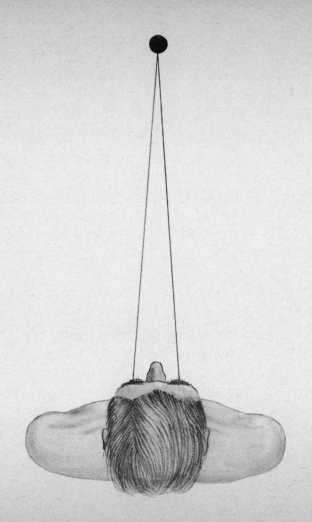

Visual concentration
(eyes focusing sharply)

26

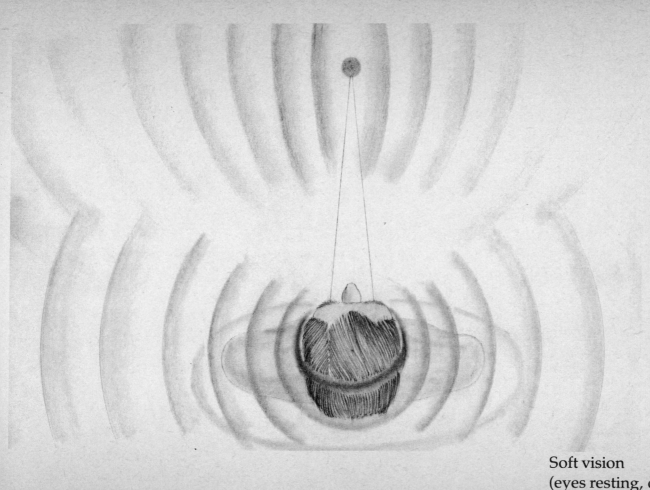

Soft vision
(eyes resting, overall
awareness)

The softer your vision is, the slower your thoughts will become. Quietness settles in. In my experience, as my perception softens, my awareness heightens. Less and less escapes it and there is less strain on the senses.

To begin with, the use of the hands is helpful but, once the principle has been understood, they are no longer necessary.

In my view, this exercise is the most basic and most vital for players of the Glass Bead Game. Like all the other exercises, it is for relaxation. Most people have learned to latch compulsively onto objects and details with their eyes and to focus sharply all the time. Few of us are aware that the thoughts in our heads are doing exactly the same thing, rushing from detail to detail, without ever comprehending the whole.

We must first become aware of the compulsive way in which we focus our eyes and thoughts before we can learn to relax the intensity of our grip. This is the purpose of the second exercise.

Looking nowhere – seeing everything

He maintained a calm, distant aloofness from the people and their activities, yet gave the feeling of complete awareness of present, past and future events. [17]

Raise a finger at arm's length into the air in front of your eyes. Let your gaze rest on the finger. After a while, take the finger away quite quickly, either sideways or downwards. But let the focus of your eyes remain exactly at the point in space where your finger was. To start with, it is not easy to keep your eyes focused exactly as they were. Having nothing to focus on anymore, they will inevitably try to focus on a further detail, the next object, along the line of vision. The focus of your eyes will want to jump to the next point in space offering a clearly defined picture.

Only after practising for a while using your finger will you be able to leave your eyes focused on Nothing. You will succeed only if you do it without forcing, without straining. Any headache, nausea, or similar symptom is a sign of tension. However, when your eyes – soft-focused – come to rest on Nothing, when they cease to be subject to the urge to latch onto the next object, then a clear calm will make itself felt which not only benefits the eyes but equally the spirit.

As in the previous exercise, everything within an angle of up to 210° can be seen but no one thing is particularly important. In this way, it is possible to keep your calmness and clarity, and not lose your 'centre', even amid the greatest of turmoil.

These first two exercises are not restricted to any particular place or time. They can be practised in any everyday situation. In due course, you will come to understand that what you are doing is not 'gymnastics for the eyes' but a mental/spiritual practice. When this lesson – through your conscious experience – has become quite clear to you, when your eyes and your mind have learned to relax consciously at any time, then a big step has been taken. The following exercises will refine this ability even more.

Double thumbs

If you use your mind to work on your mind, how can you possibly avoid a tremendous confusion?[18]

Hold both thumbs upright in front of your face, one at arm's length, the other at half that distance. They should be in line with the tip of your nose. Here again, we are concerned with separating conscious awareness from vision itself.

First, focus your eyes on the farthest thumb. While your eyes remain focused there, allow your attention to detach itself from your point of focus and let it widen until it embraces your entire visual field, particularly the thumb closer to your eyes. This thumb will be seen as a double image. In other words, since it is much closer to the eyes than the other one (which is in focus), the image perceived by the right eye will be seen as separate from the image seen by the left eye. By closing your eyes alternately, you can easily discern any differentiation in visual acuity between the two eyes.

The double image will never be absolutely sharp. And people who have one eye dominant may take some time before they can see the other eye's image at all. Since spatial – or three-dimensional – vision depends directly on the ability to perceive the images of both eyes and to merge them in the brain, this exercise is specially important for those with difficulties in respect of spatial perception.

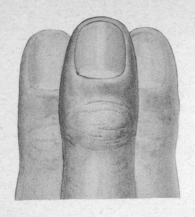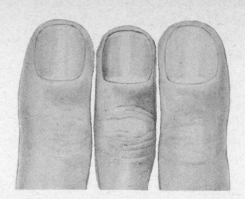

The next step is to shift the focus to the thumb nearer the eyes. This now makes the thumb which is further away appear as a double image. By looking alternately from one thumb to the other – always with the same relaxed attentiveness – the eyes will learn to concentrate easily on an object which, while being in the line of vision, is not at the point of focus. In this way, you learn how to perceive something clearly without *fixing* your attention on it.

It thus becomes apparent that in these exercises we are essentially concerned with observing our vision – not our thumbs.

One double thumb

'My predilection is to see,' he said.
'What do you mean by that?'
'I like to see,' he said, 'because only by seeing
can a man of knowledge know.' [19]

You now need only one thumb, the one further away. Your eyes rest on it, giving you one simple, sharp image. Now move your point of focus away from the thumb and closer to the eyes, roughly to where the second thumb was in the previous exercise; the image will again become double. The difficulty is that the thumb which previously served as a guide is no longer there and you are now focusing in empty space (as in the second exercise, 'Looking nowhere – seeing everything').

With your eyes focused on this Nothing, maintain your relaxed awareness of the double image. To begin with, it is quite normal for the eyes to keep shifting back and forth in a restless way. They need time to become accustomed to this practice of detached vision. If you experience signs of fatigue, it is advisable to stop and try again later, or the next day. You are not trying to train your eyes by force. It is as if – instead of following the familiar, single, straight line of your brain – you are discovering the sidetracks and crossroads, tracing new shapes, curves and patterns. This takes time. But, as your vision relaxes, a feeling of ease will settle in – a feeling which is unmistakable.

Given time, it will become easy to shift the focus gently away from the thumb and to 'squint' into the empty space between thumb and nose. It is interesting that in our culture the ability to focus in the near distance is regarded as desirable when directed at a definite object, whereas to keep the eyes in the same focus without looking at anything in particular is considered unnatural – even as a bad habit clearly in need of correction. Squinting is more or less taboo.

Many people doing these exercises for the first time are faced with this taboo and it can be a great hindrance at the beginning.

You are now gently shifting your point of focus from the thumb to a closer point where there is Nothing to be seen, and back again. The distance of the thumb from the eyes can be changed as desired. A further double image emerges if you focus on a point beyond the thumb (where, again, there may be Nothing to be seen). To begin with, there may be some difficulty in differentiating between the two double images. However, the more you become aware of the eyes' activity, the easier it will be to distinguish between the different double images. The transitions become increasingly fluid and the exercise becomes a relaxed (and relaxing) game.

Exercise for the weaker (non-dominant) eye

'I can see nobody on the road,' said Alice.
'I only wish I had such eyes,' the King remarked in a fretful tone. 'To be able to see Nobody! And at that distance too! Why, it's as much as I can do to see real people, by this light!' [20]

Here is another exercise using one thumb only. (It does not necessarily have to be a thumb; a pencil, candle or any other object which happens to be at hand may be used. For this exercise, it is best if the contours are as sharply defined as possible.)

Find the distance at which you can read clearly with the least strain on your eyes. Hold the thumb up at that distance so that you can focus on it.

Close your eyes alternately and compare the images. Is one sharper than the other? Which one? If there is a distinguishable difference, is it possible to adjust the blurred image? Can you focus the weaker eye separately at the distance of the thumb?

If the eyes shift into a squint, giving a double image, are both images equally clear? Or does the weaker (lazier) eye slip out of focus? If this happens and one of the images blurs, direct your attention to that weaker image – without changing the squint – and try to adjust the focus of that eye independently of the other eye (which remains open throughout).

This is one of the most difficult exercises, especially if – as in my own case – the two eyes show very different temperaments. However, it is also one of the most rewarding if you succeed in gaining some conscious control over the various eye muscles. This exercise should not be practised late at night when the eyes are tired (even though the muscles may then be more relaxed). Relaxation is important, but it must be conscious relaxation when the muscles are not tired, so that the entire, active muscle movement can be fully experienced. Only then can conscious control be properly gained over it.

Once you are able to do this exercise with a slight squint, go on to do it with your eyes in a distant-focus position, i.e. look beyond the thumb.

The further away from the object you look – i.e. the further apart the two components of the double image move away from each other – the more difficult the exercise becomes. So bear in mind, it is quite sufficient that you are able to do it with only a small deviation. You are not concerned with achieving the most difficult feat possible but with learning to see consciously. It is enough that you have consciously experienced a few times the action of the muscles. Once acquired, this capacity will never be lost.

Four thumbs

No longer is there any central point which might be seen.[21]

Hold both thumbs upright and parallel at a 'reading distance' of about a foot to sixteen inches (30–40 cms) in front of you and two to four inches (5–10 cms) apart. Make sure that the lighting is adequate and similar for both thumbs. Let the eyes go into a squint (looking at Nothing) so that the thumbs double up and four thumbs are seen. The four thumbs appear spatially separate and transparent because each one of them is seen by one eye only, whilst the other eye has a clear field of vision at that point.

This exercise consists in following the outlines of the four thumbs visually without allowing the fourfold image to slip. This is quite possible if the eyes are relaxed. The more relaxed they are in following the outlines, the clearer the contours and details of each thumb will appear.

The dominant eye will present no great difficulties. However, the weaker one will only be able to maintain a clear image once there is consciousness of the chronic tensions in the eye muscles and they begin to relax. Depending on how often you practise, and the state of your eyes, this may take anything from a few minutes to several weeks to accomplish. This exercise should also be done in a playful way, frequently, and for a short time only – not more than three minutes at a time initially. Not only will your eyes become tense and tired through struggling against resistance but the brain, which is the real target of the exercise, needs time to adjust to this unaccustomed way of looking. Eventually, it will become easy to gain a clear image of all four thumbs. The following exercises are based on this ability.

The middle thumb

It is that our normal waking consciousness, rational consciousness as we call it, is but one special type of consciousness, whilst all about it, parted from it by the flimsiest of screens, lie potential forms of consciousness entirely different.[22]

The thumbs should be in the same position as in the last exercise – upright, parallel and about two inches apart, at reading-distance or a little further away. Again, squint at Nothing so that you obtain four separate images. Now shift your squint in such a way that the two inner thumbs overlap more and more until they cover each other completely. If they were not quite parallel to begin with, or if they are unevenly illuminated, correct as appropriate.

The middle thumb which thus emerges is a composite image: the right eye is seeing the left thumb, the left eye the right thumb. The two together give this image of a thumb which does not exist. Furthermore, you will be seeing it in a place where you know there is Nothing.

With practice, this image will become clear, extremely clear. A small black dot painted in the centre of each thumb-nail makes it easier to bring the two images together in a relaxed way. The two outside thumbs can still be seen to the right and left of the middle thumb; they are considerably less clear, and are transparent as before. Only the middle thumb appears to be 'real'.

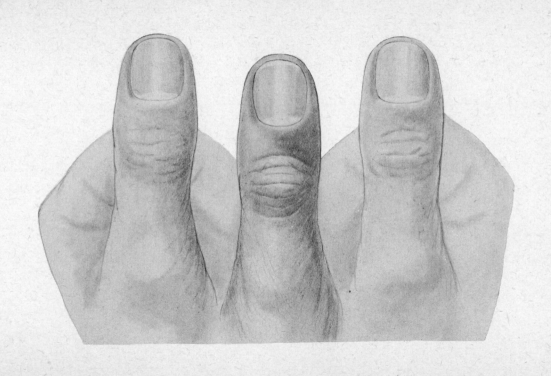

Nothing is more magnificent than precious stones and gold, nothing finer than a diamond, nothing more noble than the blood of kings. Nothing is holy in war. Nothing is higher than heaven. Nothing is deeper than hell. Nothing is more glorious than virtue . . .[23]

In this exercise again, it is the brain which has the most difficult task to perform. It is receiving an image of Something from a place where there is Nothing! The thumb which is perceiving in this way does not exist in the brain's accustomed reality, especially as it is a kind of hermaphrodite, consisting half of the right thumb and half of the left.

Instead of thumbs – which have the advantage of always being handy, but with the disadvantage that they are frequently quite dissimilar, thus making it difficult to overlap them well – you can of course use pencils, coins, stamps or similar objects.

Large thumb – small thumb

My Drawing Number One. It looked like this:

I showed my masterpiece to the grown-ups, and asked them whether the drawing frightened them.

But they answered: 'Frighten? Why should anyone be frightened by a hat?'

My drawing was not a picture of a hat. It was a picture of a boa constrictor digesting an elephant. But since the grown-ups were not able to understand it, I made another drawing: I drew the inside of the boa constrictor, so that the grown-ups could see it clearly. They always need to have things explained.

My Drawing Number Two looked like this:[24]

In the previous exercise, we reached a plane which – by our normal standards – is unreal. Now it will become clear that this plane is governed by different laws from those of our so-called 'real' world. In this real world we find it quite natural for an object to appear larger the closer it is to us. It seems logical and can be explained in scientific terms.

This is not the case in our newly-found 'unreal' world. On the contrary, the closer an object seems to be the smaller it becomes.

When you are able to maintain a clear image of the middle thumb (pencil or whatever) in a relaxed way, slowly move the hands apart and back together again.

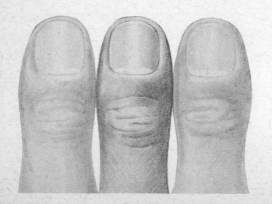   

To begin with, the image will tend to resolve itself into its various parts – on the one hand because it is difficult to keep sight of Something in Nothing and, on the other hand, because the eyes have yet to learn to follow the counter-directional movements (the right eye to the left, the left eye to the right). After a while it becomes quite easy; the eyes hold the image without any strain, even during the movement.

Something peculiar happens. When the thumbs are moved apart, the image of the middle thumb appears to move through space, coming closer. And when the thumbs are brought together again, it seems to drift further away. And the closer the middle thumb comes towards you, the smaller it gets!

This exercise should be practised sparingly, especially at the beginning. The more successfully your eyes have learned to see in a relaxed way through doing the previous exercises, the easier it will be to hold the image of the middle thumb without strain. In order to achieve this, it is important that you do not simply follow the exercises rigidly. You must gain your own understanding of them from your experience. You have to lay down the new pathways in your brain yourself, one by one, before you can put them to effective use.

Red circle – blue circle

The find-out, it has last me my whole life. In a way I was always hopping back and forth across the boundary line of the mind. [25]

Having succeeded in overlapping two similar objects, we can now start doing so with different ones. Most stationers sell plain, round stickers in various sizes and colours. They are excellent for this exercise.

Stick one red and one blue (about an inch in diameter) on a white sheet of paper, about an inch or two apart. At reading-distance, the illustration on the next page is ideal. Larger circles may be used – at a correspondingly larger distance apart.

By squinting, double up the images of the two circles and bring the inner red circle onto the inner blue circle, overlapping them perfectly. This will take some time. In the beginning, the images will tend to slip apart before a clear red/blue image can be established in the middle. It is most important not to fight against the tendency of the central image to disintegrate and jump around. Just let it happen. Eventually, the contours will – almost automatically – become sharp and clear. Practice of the fifth exercise (Exercise for the weaker – non-dominant – eye) will make it easier to focus each eye separately on the image of the inner circles. As before with the thumbs, the outlines of the two inner circles may tend to blur as they come closer together; but, with patience and relaxation, you will soon be able to keep them sharp as you bring them together and finally succeed in merging them into one.

When you can look at the central red/blue circle for longer periods and can follow its contours without strain, a mental calmness will settle in – a calmness which fully

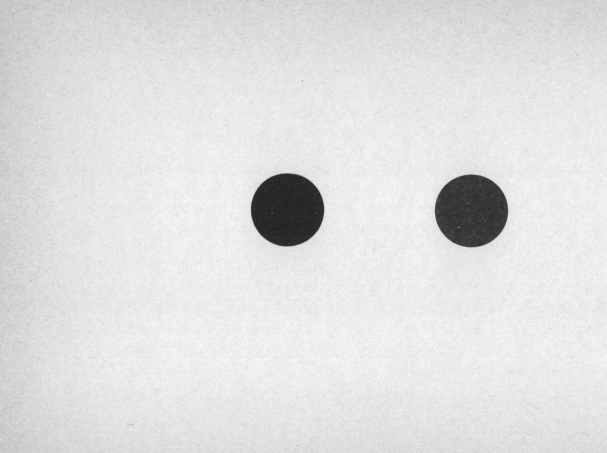

corresponds with the relaxed state of your eyes. Again it is clear that our mental state is directly connected with the way in which we use our eyes. Now we shall examine this relationship the other way round – thinking is affected by seeing but seeing is also directly influenced by thought. The purpose of this exercise is to allow you to experience this for yourself.

You only need to think 'Now I am seeing the middle circle *red*' for the eye which is seeing the red circle to become dominant – which is to say that the blue element of the image will give way to the red. When you switch the thought to 'Now I am seeing it *blue*', the red image will give way to the blue one; i.e. the other eye will become dominant.

It will feel as though you are throwing subtle switches in your brain. And you will soon find it quite easy to do. You can truly decide what you want to see – blue with one eye dominant, red with the other dominant, or red/blue by finding the balance, the point of calmness.

This exercise is not merely an entertaining and informative game whereby you can learn a great deal about the connection between seeing and thinking. It is also an excellent meditation enabling you to find a visual and mental resting place – centered and balanced within yourself. (cf. Contemplation of the Ten Thousand Things, p. 63.)

Three-dimensional vision –
for those who do not know it

Is the world a dream?
Is it of substance, pray tell! —
Neither of substance
Nor yet a dream to my knowledge:
A Something, a Nothing in one.[26]

I have noticed that many left-handed people who have been trained to use their right hands have difficulty in connecting the images seen by their two eyes to form a single three-dimensional picture in the brain. It is as if a wall has been set up in the brain to separate the two images. Thus objects are seen only with the dominant eye, while the images seen with the other eye remain below the level of awareness – behind the wall. This then means that the middle thumb or circle is not seen by them as floating in space but as being on the same plane as the outer ones. And, in the 'Red circle – blue circle' exercise, a clear preference for one of the two images (colours) is experienced.

The following exercise is a further step towards three-dimensional vision, particularly helpful for 'converted' left-handers.

Start as you did in 'Red circle – blue circle'. If the middle circle appears to be on the same plane as the other two – and only of one colour – you can gain access to the other colour by repeatedly covering up the dominant eye. It is important that you become able to see both colours, even if the image remains flat, in one plane.

Now hold a finger up close in front of your nose where – with relaxed attention – you will see it as a double image. (If the finger has too little contrast, use a candle flame instead.) Your eyes continue to rest on the middle circle.

Slowly move the finger away from your nose towards the circle and allow your attention to follow its double image. The two images of your finger (or candle flame) will come closer together the further the finger (or candle flame) is moved away from your nose, until, finally, somewhere in the space between nose and paper, they become united. This is the point at which the middle circle appears to 'float' for people with normal vision. At this point, both the middle circle and the visual aid (finger or candle flame) are seen as single, composite, sharply outlined images. (It may help to cover the two outer circles, which are on the same plane as that of the middle image, i.e. halfway between nose and paper.)

This is a rewarding exercise which – depending on the amount of damage suffered previously – will require great relaxation, inner awareness and patience.

Curved space

Truly I am a happy man:
Whenever I wish, I seek out the pure land,
Being there and being here,
Being there and being here,
There and here.
Namu-amida-butsu! Namu-amida-butsu! [10]

The middle circle appears to float high above the paper. It is also a little smaller than the two outer ones. Its floating quality becomes strikingly apparent if you attempt to touch it with your finger. In this way, you can determine the exact height at which it is floating. (The extraordinary nature of the floating red/blue circle becomes even more apparent when the two outer circles are covered – at the floating level.)

If you have repeatedly and successfully done the previous exercises, your eyes will find it easy to hold the image of the middle circle, in a relaxed state and without any strain.

This can easily be tested by closing the eyes for a while. If the image is still sharp and floating when you open your eyes again, then your eyes and mind are relaxed. This state of quiet relaxation is comparable to that of a bird which, whilst sleeping on one leg, can remain steadily upright on a branch which is moving in the wind, without the slightest strain or difficulty.[27]

When you have reached this state, you can let your eyes wander away from the floating circle whilst, at the same time, keeping its image absolutely sharp. Your eyes maintain exactly the same focal distance as before. In order to test whether this is really the case, return the eyes to the floating circle from time to time. If it is still sharp and the colours still cover each other exactly so that there is no need to adjust them, then the eyes have remained relaxed (and the mind also). Your eyes will be able to roam through empty space in ever-increasing orbits. Since the tension and relaxation of your eyes is connected with your mental state, be sure to do this exercise – in which your eyes do not latch onto anything anymore – in a playful, purposeless way.

The plane on which the red/blue circle floats will begin to become substantial. Your eyes will follow it like a pane of glass. It is an arched plane. The empty space in which your eyes are wandering will appear to curve towards you all around, and to be more dense at that distance than elsewhere. It is a strange feeling to have given the Nothing a visible/invisible form.

However, take care. The slightest enthusiasm or fascination arising in your mind will destroy the image, shattering the invisible plane, causing your eyes to slip into another focus.

> It demands an attitude which occurs in life only under very specific, rare circumstances: a state of utmost detachment of mind and soul from the visual experience.[28]

Hints

Anyone wishing to go beyond the exercises given in this book and to delve into Contemplation of the Ten Thousand Things may refer to Pierre Derlon's work.[12] Derlon was initiated by French gipsies into some of their secret traditions and was given permission to publish them.

He describes a form of visual contemplation in which two circles, two squares and two rectangles (ratio 2:1) – one of each pair being red and the other blue – are brought together by squinting, in such a way that a threefold double image appears in the middle. (The illustration opposite, used by Derlon, is an artist's impression of the practice.)

The shape, colour and arrangement of the figures is closely connected with designs in Gothic architecture and to the legend of The Holy Grail. Those who are interested in this aspect will find many references in Louis Charpentier's *The Mysteries of Chartres Cathedral.*[29]

It is interesting and typical that Derlon does not state what this meditation is ultimately about, what one 'sees' when looking at the images. Our literary heritage is full of hints that there *is* something to 'see'; but it never states what it is.

61

Here is a particularly good example of this:

(I) . . . brought out the carbon crystal with great eagerness and held one of its darkly-mirroring facets towards the moonlight. The reflections that issued from it were a blueish, sheer black-violet, and for some time thereafter I could discover nothing more from it apart from this observation. But at the same time there grew up within me a wonderful peace which was corporeally tangible, and the black crystal in my hand ceased to tremble, for my fingers had become firm and sure, as had every aspect of myself.

Then the moonlight on the crystal became iridescent. Milky, opaline veils of cloud arose upon it, and subsided again. At length an outlined image stood out distinctly from the mirroring surface, so tiny to start with, like gnomes playing in the clear moonlight, observed as it were through a spy-hole. Soon, however, the images began to increase, in both breadth and depth, and what I saw became — spaceless, yet just as substantial as if I myself were in the midst of it. And I saw . . . (Here the manuscript was burnt.)[30]

It makes no difference whether we use a carbon crystal, a crystal ball, gipsy figurations, stones, shadows or circles. What is essential is the way in which we look at them.

Contemplation of the Ten Thousand Things

Those who have worked seriously on themselves for a while with the help of these exercises will have noticed that they can give access to an abundance of unusual, beautiful and sometimes disturbing experiences.

Here I feel at odds with myself. There is a temptation to say many things as to the whys and wherefores. I would like to tell beginners of the Glass Bead Game about the essentials, explain the practice of the Game. I would like to give them aids on the Way, to point out the pitfalls which occur – particularly at the beginning – to give additional exercises, to tell of my experiences and those of others . . .

However, I will not do any of these things.

The true Glass Bead Game unfolds in the course of practice – for each player in his own way and in his own time. It evolves from Contemplation of the Ten Thousand Things.

Cut two circles of coloured card – one red, one blue.
Lay them on the floor or stick them on the wall.
Sit in front of them
– and look!

> Whatever you see –
> > look at it, but do not stop there;
> > it is only one of the ten thousand things.
> Whatever you feel –
> > feel it, but do not stop there;
> > it is only one of the ten thousand things.
> Whatever you think –
> > think it, but do not stop there;
> > it is only one of the ten thousand things.

> For only where there seems to be a duality, there one sees another, one feels another,
> one smells another's perfume, one tastes another, one speaks to another, one listens
> to another, one touches another and one knows another.

> But in the ocean of Spirit, the seer is alone beholding his own immensity.[31]

2 + 2

A Glass Bead Game for Beginners

That which we are accustomed to call 'mathematics' is nothing but a random conglomeration of rules for a clearly defined and very limited plane of communication.

What follows is an expansion of these rules – an expansion of our communication onto other planes.

Those who prefer to stick to the conventional rules will be perfectly correct in maintaining that this Game is nonsense. But life does not stick to rules – except perhaps to that one!

Take a look at this formula – which has probably governed your life until today:

$$2 + 2 = 4$$

If you allow yourself to get involved in this Game, you will never again be able to see this formula in the way you see it today. For the player of the Glass Bead Game, it is merely one of an infinite number of possible ideas.

Let us celebrate for one last time the familiar calculation on which this formula is based:

If I have two apples in my left hand, and two apples in my right, how many apples do I have altogether?

This ritual has reigned over our world until today. Let us bid it farewell. We are moving on.

Take a look at these two apples:

Now close your left eye. How many apples do you see with your right eye?

Now open your left eye again and close the right one. How many apples can you see with your left eye?

Two both times? Good. Now we will put two and two together again.

Open both eyes.

How many apples do you see?

You can say it out loud as you learned to say it at school:

> *I see two apples with my left eye and two apples with my right. How many apples do I see altogether?*

If you are still unable to see more than two apples, you have succeeded – by the simplest of means – in reaching a new plane of reality where

$$2 + 2 = 2$$

The circumstance which makes this plane essentially different from the abstract mathematical one is the introduction of a living dimension – the fact that we are *looking*. (Remember quantum theory?)

This plane does not contradict the other one. It is complementary to it. The formula $2 + 2 = 4$ is equally valid here, as can easily be demonstrated:

Hold up your index finger – at about a quarter of the distance from the tip of your nose to the apples (on the opposite page) – without obscuring them from view. Look at it with both eyes. You should be able to see a simple and clear image of the finger.

Close your left eye and look at your finger with the right. Now detach your attention from your point of focus (which is still the finger) and transfer it to the (slightly blurred) apples in the background.

You will see two apples, slightly to the right of your finger. Correct?

Now open your left eye and close the right. Two apples again, a little to the left of the finger this time.

Alternate, closing first one and then the other eye, allowing the apples to jump to and fro for a while. Make sure that your point of focus remains on the finger while you do it. (Once you have learned the trick, you can do it without the finger.)

It is important that you succeed in seeing the left eye's image separately from the right eye's image. Mathematicians all over the world will sleep a great deal easier if you succeed!

Here are two more apples – for practice.

Now comes the most important part: open both eyes at the same time – still focusing on the finger. Give attention to the apples in the background. Of course, they are a fair distance beyond your point of focus – and are therefore a little blurred; but that does not matter.

How many are there?

Two apples to the right of the finger, two to the left.

Quod erat demonstrandum . . . on this plane, too:

$$2 + 2 = 4$$

Now, take care! This will not be easy the first time.

Your task is now to bring the inner two of the four apples together so that they fully cover each other. You will have to learn to shift your point of focus around in empty space – but, until you can do that easily, you can use the tip of your index finger to help you.

Look at your finger-tip with both eyes and move it slowly backwards and forwards between your nose and the apples until you can see only three apples in the background – that is, until the two inner apples merge into one.

The apples may shift to and fro for a while before the (composite) one in the middle becomes quite sharp and clear. Then you can take the finger away.

Do *not* strain your eyes. You can only succeed if they are fully relaxed.

So, now count how many apples there are this time. You will find the answer on the next page.

$$2 + 2 = 3$$

Now there are three apples.

You will also notice that the one in the middle is not only a little smaller than the outer ones but that it also seems to float in mid-air – roughly at the point where your finger was while you were practising. Furthermore, this central apple is clearer and better defined than the other two.

What a paradox!

The apple which can be seen most clearly does not exist. It is without substance. From another world. You can put your finger close to the place where the apple seems to be floating, but you cannot touch it.

Look at it for a while.

When you have found the right distance and your eyes have come to rest on the central apple, the two outer ones will start to grow fainter in your perception – and you will understand why, on this plane of reality, it is quite valid to say:

$$2 + 2 = 1$$

Let us now take squares instead of apples.

Look at them and repeat the steps you have been through up to now: from $2 + 2 = 2$ to $2 + 2 = 4$ and on to $2 + 2 = 3/1$.

You see, it not only works with apples!

Now shift your point of focus a little closer towards the squares – further away from your eyes.

You will obtain a new version of $2 + 2 = 4$, looking somewhat like this:

Allow your eyes to become gradually accustomed to this new way of looking. Give them time to settle down in this new 'in between' space. If you try too hard, you may become dizzy and your eyes will begin to hurt. Just relax into it.

When the new image has become clear, with the correct spacings and overlaps, look how many squares there are to be seen in all.

You will find four large ones and, in addition to them, three smaller ones resulting from the overlaps. They have a luminosity of their own which distinguishes them from the large ones.

You can change the size of these smaller squares by squinting either a little more or a little less. But, no matter how you look into this 'in between' space, you will always have these three additional squares which have appeared from another plane of reality – a reality in which the Weights and Measures Act clearly becomes relative:

$$2 + 2 = 7$$

Don't forget: you are still seeing two images with the left eye and two with the right. The basis of this Glass Bead Game is still $2 + 2$.

Let us now give the squares different colours – the left one red and the right one blue.

Repeat the process which led to 2 + 2 = 7 and observe the colours – colour being yet another plane of reality.

We started off with two colours – red and blue. Now we have five:

> Transparent blue (2 squares)
> Transparent red (2 squares)
> Intensive blue (1 square)
> Intensive red (1 square)
> Blue/red (1 square)

Our new discovery:

$$2 + 2 = 5$$

There are other ways to arrive at 2 + 2 = 5. We can, for instance, arrange two squares of the same colour vertically.

You will observe that we are now introducing what we may call 'the negative'. The negative or 'non-square', which appears in the middle of the other four squares, is in a relationship to them similar to that of the electron to the positron, or of anti-matter to matter.

Polarity is born.

Try another example. Arrange the squares in another way – turning the vertical squares through an angle of 45°.

If you double them up, they will form a zig-zag pattern – one up, one down, one up, one down. Observe the negative squares. Depending on how *you decide* to see them, you will obtain different results.

Either you will see four squares and four negative squares – which gives:

$$2 + 2 = 8$$

Or, if you define only those squares as negative which are clearly enclosed on at least three sides, then the four squares plus two negative squares will give:

$$2 + 2 = 6$$

You can also amuse yourself by cancelling out the negative squares (or apples) against the positive ones. With eight squares, that will make $2 + 2 \, (= 4 - 4) = 0$; i.e.

$$2 + 2 = 0$$

And with six squares, you will again find

$$2 + 2 = 2$$

Thus you can see that, depending on which rules have been agreed on, you can arrive at the most varied and surprising results. Within the framework of the rules chosen, these results are no less valid than the familiar

$$2 + 2 = 4$$

While we are at this point, take another look at our hitherto unquestionable 'truth'.

Take time to allow this familiar formula to sink into your mind again.

$$2 + 2 = 4$$

Do you notice any difference?

If you meditate on the various numbers, you will become aware that each of them is absolute in itself, and that each has a dynamic quality of its own. $2 + 2 = 8$, for example, has a totally different quality from $2 + 2 = 3$, whilst the 7 and the 5 are quite similar. These subtle qualities are difficult to describe in words but, as objects of meditation, they are inexhaustible.

Have you tried doing it with
five apples yet?

To start with, squares are easier. But you will find that the negative apple is – on this plane of observation – just as real as the negative square.

Like this!

94

You begin to suspect that there is no end to this Game.
Exactly!

Instead of squares and apples, let us now, for simplicity's sake, use imaginary glass beads. We will arrange them vertically.

Now we are going to expand the Game beyond the two dimensions of the page – to include the whole universe.

Double the beads. (2 + 2 = 4)

Add the concept of polarity, introducing a negative glass bead in the middle.

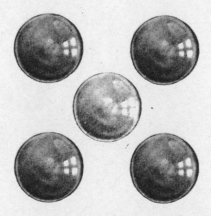

If you expand your field of vision, you will observe four additional spaces at the periphery of the configuration – spaces which could also hold negative beads.

These spaces are not as clearly defined as the one in the middle. You can conclude from this that four such negative beads in these spaces would be slightly less clear or smaller.

The new figure would look something like this:

You could read it as:

$$2 + 2 = 9$$

or as:

$$2 + 2 = -1$$

if you cancel out the positive glass beads against the negative.

At this point, you may introduce three-dimensional vision. Do so with your inner eye, with your imagination.

Start with the four positive beads and imagine their negative satellites (as on the opposite page). Imagine that the four outer, negative beads – because of their less clearly defined space – are not just less clear, or smaller, but that they are further away.

Now the image has become spatial, three-dimensional. The four positive beads lie in one plane; the four outer, negative ones lie on another, further away. You can imagine the central bead to be wherever you like – either out in front of, or a little behind the positive ones, just as you wish.

It is not difficult to conjure up this three-dimensional image before the inner eye. Of course, at the moment you can only see one side of the whole image. But if you stretch your imagination around the edges of the configuration, you can catch a glimpse of the rest of it. . .

It will consist of as many glass beads – positive and negative – as you care to imagine.

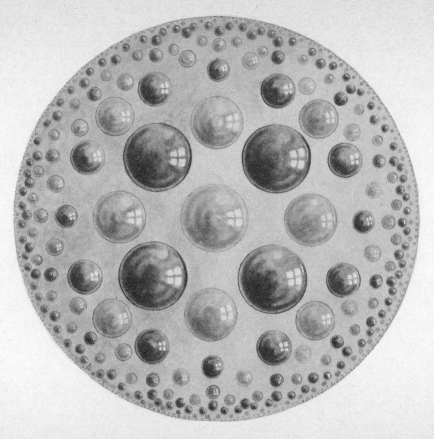

Go on, then, to imagine what this construction looks like inside. Move round the interior and observe it carefully. When you are able to see the inner structure, and the relationships between the glass beads, you will discover that you are looking at nothing less than the three-dimensional grid of a crystal – the very blueprint and foundation of creation and life.

I have accompanied you thus far. Now I must leave the rest of the Game to you and your imagination.

Words cannot convey the infinite, but the mind can experience it. Your mind. Everybody's mind. It is only that we are not aware of it. Ordinarily, we restrict ourselves to the conventional formula: $2 + 2 = 4$ – and we believe this to be the only 'truth'.

It is not so!

'. . . When knowledge has passed through the infinite, grace returns; and in such a way that, at the same time, it appears most pure in that human frame which has no awareness or infinite awareness — that is to say, in the puppet or in the god.'

   'And so,' I said, somewhat bewildered, 'would we have to eat again of the Tree of Knowledge in order to return to a state of innocence?'

   'Indeed,' he replied. 'That is the last chapter in the history of the world.'[11]

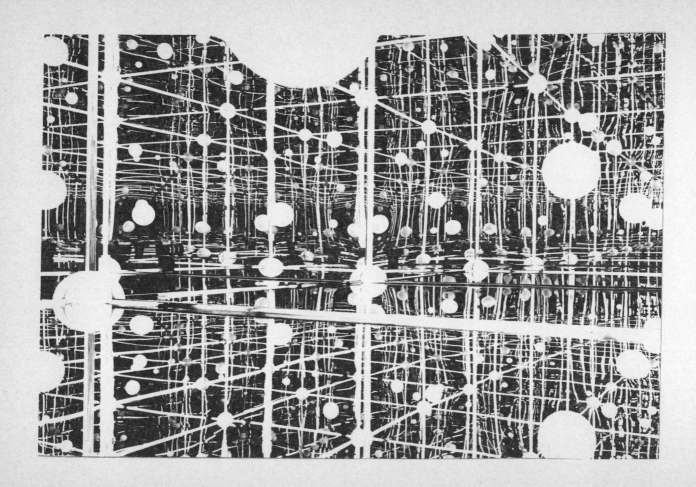

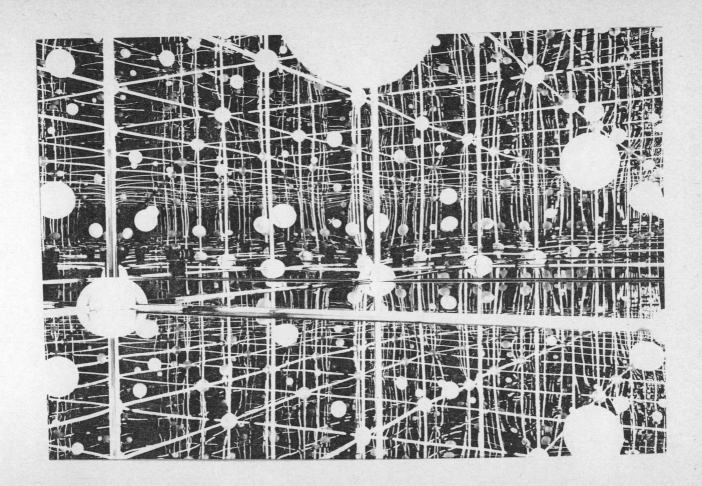

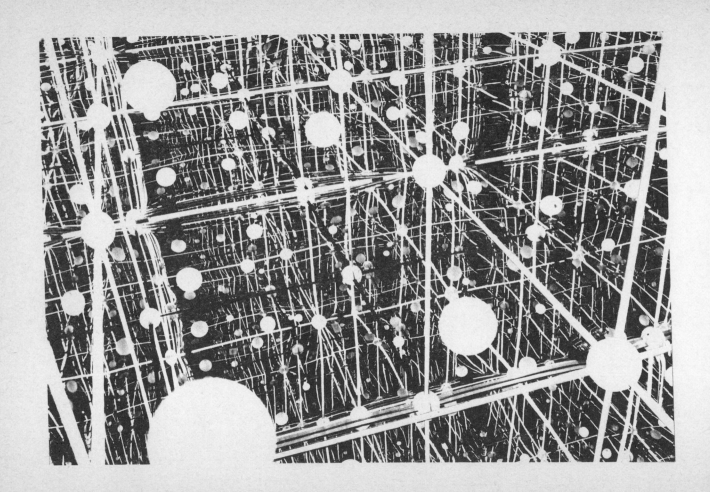

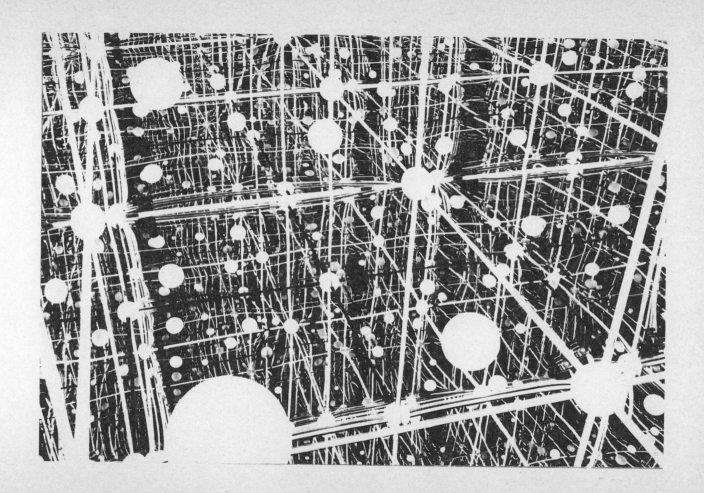

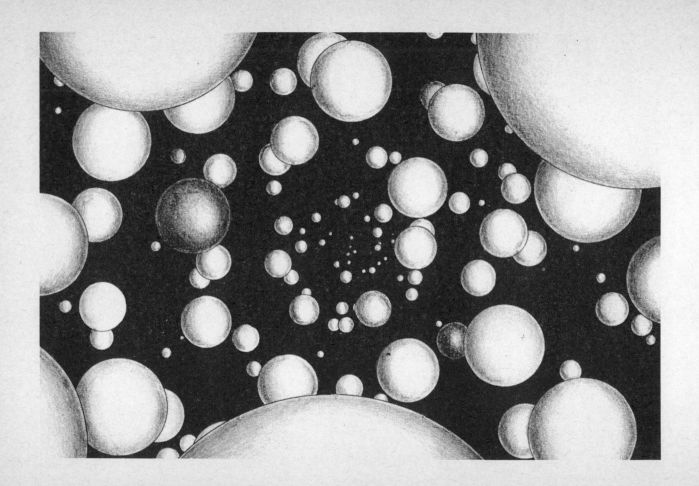

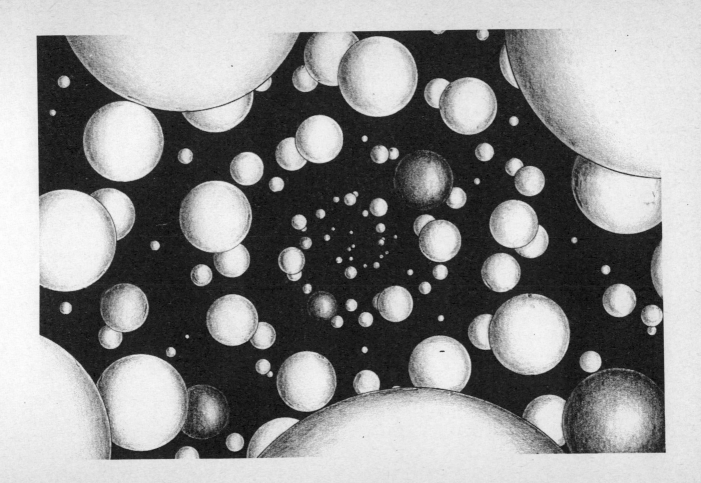

Notes and references

1 – Lao Tzu, *Tao Te Ching*, tr. Gia Fu Feng and Jane English, Random House, New York, 1972.

2 – Hermann Hesse, *The Glass Bead Game*, Penguin Modern Classics, 1972.

3 – *Holy Bible* (A.V.), Gen. 3:4, 5.

4 – The legend of The Holy Grail – standing symbolically for the search for mystical reunion with God – describes this in remarkably rich imagery. (See 29.)

5 – In this context, it is interesting that Humanistic Psychology, which has gained much importance over the past two decades, was originally called the Human Potential Movement. It is essentially concerned with evolution along this path and the development of techniques to this end. Active Evolution is the title of a workshop series which I offer in Germany to those wishing to work actively in this direction. (c/o Coloman Institut, 8091 Soyen, W. Germany.)

6 – Kaushitaki Upanishad, 3:8. Quoted from *The Upanishads*, tr. Juan Mascaró, Penguin Classics, 1965.

7 – Mircea Eliade, *Shamanism; Archaic Techniques of Ecstasy*, Routledge, London, 1964. Princeton University Press, 1972.

8 – Michael Ende, *Die Unendliche Geschichte*, Thienmanns, Stuttgart, 1979.

9 – Alan Watts, *The Way of Zen*, Thames & Hudson, London, 1957.

10 – From Saichi's writings, quoted in D. T. Suzuki's *Der Westliche und der Östliche Weg*, Ullstein, 1971.

11 – Heinrich von Kleist, *Über das Marionettentheater*, ro ro ro Klassiker Verlag, 1964.

12 – Pierre Derlon, *Secrets Oubliés des Derniers Initiés Gitans*, Éditions Robert Laffont, Paris, 1977. The illustration on p. 61 is by Yves Derlon.

13 – Henry Miller, *The Smile at the Foot of the Ladder*, Village Press, London, 1973. New Directions, U.S.A.

14 – Carlos Castaneda, *Journey to Ixtlan*, The Bodley Head, London, 1972.

15 – Carlos Castaneda, *Tales of Power*, Hodder & Stoughton, London, 1975. Simon & Schuster, New York, 1974.

16 – Those who wear glasses which limit their field of vision may include the glasses themselves in their widening perception – the frames, the parts leading back to the ears, their pressure on the nose and behind the ears, etc.

17 – Manuel Córdova-Rios writing about the old Amahuaca chief, Xumu; quoted by Joan Halifax in *Shamanic Voices*, Penguin, 1980. E. P. Dutton, New York, 1979.

18 – Seng-Ts'an quoted by P. Hughes and G. Brecht in *Vicious Circles and Infinity*, Jonathan Cape, London, 1975.

19 – Carlos Castaneda, *A Separate Reality*, The Bodley Head, London, 1971.

20 – Lewis Carroll, *Through the Looking-Glass*, Collins, London, 1954 (and various other editions).

21 – J. W. Goethe; quotation translated by author from *Der Verlust der Mitte*, by Hans Sedlmayr, Ullstein, 1966.

22 – William James, *The Varieties of Religious Experience*, Collins Fontana Library, 1960. Collier Macmillan, New York, 1961.

23 – Passerat (medieval author) quoted in *Vicious Circles and Infinity* (18).

24 – Antoine de Saint-Exupéry, *The Little Prince*, Pan, 1974 (and various other editions).

25 – Lame Deer, quoted in *Shamanic Voices* (17).

26 – Author's translation from *Bi-Yän-Lu*; Master Yüan-wu's transcription of the Smaragda rock-wall; Carl Hanser Verlag, Munich, 1971.

27 – The author is indebted to Dr. William H. Bates for this comparison, made in *Better Eyesight Without Glasses*, Holt, Rinehart & Winston, New York, 1940.

28 – Hans Sedlmayr in *Der Verlust der Mitte* (21) speaking of Paul Cézanne's characteristic philosophy of painting (tr. author).

29 – Louis Charpentier, *The Mysteries of Chartres Cathedral* (tr. Sir Ronald Fraser), R.I.L.K.O., London, 1972. 'Three tables bore the Grail – a round one, a square one and a rectangular one. All three have the same surface and their number is 21.'

30 – Translation from *Der Engel vom Westlichen Fenster* by Gustav Meyrink, Langen-Müller, 1975; the quotation is from the diaries of the English Elizabethan alchemist, John Dee.

31 – 'The Supreme Teaching' from *The Upanishads* (6).